Blastoff! Beginners are developed by literacy experts and educators to meet the needs of early readers. These engaging informational texts support young children as they begin reading about their world. Through simple language and high frequency words paired with crisp, colorful photos, Blastoff! Beginners launch young readers into the universe of independent reading.

Sight Words in This Book

a	find	into	one	time
about	go	is	see	to
are	have	it	the	up
at	help	look	them	
can	her	many	they	
eat	in	on	this	

This edition first published in 2023 by Bellwether Media, Inc.

No part of this publication may be reproduced in whole or in part without written permission of the publisher. For information regarding permission, write to Bellwether Media, Inc., Attention: Permissions Department, 6012 Blue Circle Drive, Minnetonka, MN 55343.

Library of Congress Cataloging-in-Publication Data
Names: Neuenfeldt, Elizabeth, author.
Title: Baby hedgehogs / by Elizabeth Neuenfeldt.
Description: Minneapolis, MN : Bellwether Media, Inc., 2023. | Series: Blastoff! beginners: Too cute! | Includes bibliographical references and index. | Audience: Ages 4-7 | Audience: Grades K-1
Identifiers: LCCN 2022036383 (print) | LCCN 2022036384 (ebook) | ISBN 9798886871081 (hardcover) | ISBN 9798886871968 (paperback) | ISBN 9798886872347 (ebook)
Subjects: LCSH: Hedgehogs--Infancy--Juvenile literature. | Hedgehogs--Juvenile literature.
Classification: LCC QL737.E753 N48 2023 (print) | LCC QL737.E753 (ebook) | DDC 599.33/21392--dc23/eng/20220729
LC record available at https://lccn.loc.gov/2022036383
LC ebook record available at https://lccn.loc.gov/2022036384

Text copyright © 2023 by Bellwether Media, Inc. BLASTOFF! BEGINNERS and associated logos are trademarks and/or registered trademarks of Bellwether Media, Inc.

Editor: Betsy Rathburn   Designer: Jeffrey Kollock

Printed in the United States of America, North Mankato, MN.

Table of Contents

A Baby Hedgehog!	4
Small and Spiny	6
Growing Up	18
Baby Hedgehog Facts	22
Glossary	23
To Learn More	24
Index	24

A Baby Hedgehog!

Look at the baby hedgehog. Hello, hoglet!

Small and Spiny

Newborn hoglets are small.
They have **spines**.
They cannot see.

newborn

Hoglets sleep in **nests**. They drink mom's milk.

nest

mom

Hoglets have many **siblings**. They cuddle!

siblings

This hoglet is one month old. Time to go outside!

Mom helps her babies find food. They eat bugs.

bug

This hoglet curled into a ball.
It is safe!

Growing Up

Hoglets grow. It takes them about six weeks to grow up.

This hoglet can live on its own. Bye, mom!

Baby Hedgehog Facts

Hedgehog Life Stages

newborn → hoglet → adult

A Day in the Life

sleep in nests

eat bugs

curl up

Glossary

nests: homes for hedgehogs

newborn: just born

siblings: brothers and sisters

spines: sharp coverings on hedgehogs

To Learn More

ON THE WEB

FACTSURFER

Factsurfer.com gives you a safe, fun way to find more information.

1. Go to www.factsurfer.com.
2. Enter "baby hedgehogs" into the search box and click 🔍.
3. Select your book cover to see a list of related content.

Index

ball, 16
bugs, 14, 15
cuddle, 10
drink, 8
eat, 14
food, 14
grow, 18
hedgehog, 4
milk, 8

mom, 8, 9, 14, 20
nests, 8
newborn, 6
outside, 12
safe, 16
siblings, 10
sleep, 8
small, 6

spines, 6, 7

The images in this book are reproduced through the courtesy of: Nynke van Holten, front cover, pp. 1, 4-5; Eric Isselee, pp. 3, 4, 6, 10, 16-17, 22 (newborn, hoglet, adult); Bradley Dymond/ Alamy, pp. 6-7; Anna Barv, p. 8; Thanisnan Sukprasert, pp. 8-9, 23 (newborn); darren sanderson photography/ Alamy, pp. 10-11; WildMedia, pp. 12-13, 23 (siblings); Robert HENNO/ Alamy, pp. 14-15; Duncan Usher/ Alamy, pp. 18-19; supakrit tirayasupasin, pp. 20-21; Karl Van Ginderdeuren/ Buiten-be/ Minden Pictures/ SuperStock, p. 22 (sleep); Twisted Pixels, p. 22 (eat); Viktor Sergeevich, p. 22 (curl); NouN/ Biosphoto/ SuperStock, p. 23 (nest); Polryaz, p. 23 (spines).